Art Revelations

Neil Morris

THE LIFE OF JESUS

ENCHANTED LION BOOKS
NEW YORK

First American Edition published in 2003 by
Enchanted Lion Books
239 Central Park West, New York, NY, 10024
Copyright © 2003 McRae Books Srl
All rights reserved
Printed and bound in Italy by Artegrafica, Verona
A CIP record is available from the Library of Congress

ISBN 1-59270-002-0

The series "Art Revelations"
was created and produced by McRae Books Srl
Borgo Santa Croce, 8 – Florence (Italy)
info@mcraebooks.com

Series Editor: Loredana Agosta
Art History consultant: Roberto Carvalho de Magalhães
Illustrations: Studio Stalio (Alessandro Cantucci,
Fabiano Fabbrucci, Andrea Morandi)
Graphic Design: Marco Nardi

above:
PIERO DELLA FRANCESCA, *Baptism*, London, The National Gallery

opposite:
JAN VAN EYCK, *The Crucifixion*, New York, The Metropolitan Museum of Art

previous page:
ANDREIJ RUBLEV, *The Trinity*, Moscow, Tretjakov State Gallery

Table of Contents

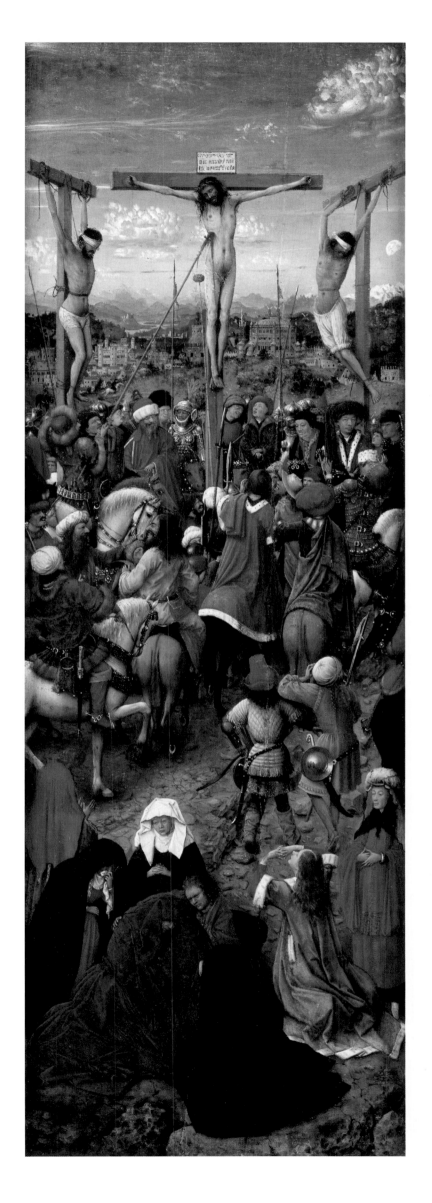

Introduction

For God so loved the world that he gave his one and only Son, that whoever believes in him shall not perish but have eternal life.

John 3:16

Christians believe that Jesus was born on earth as the Son of God and that if they follow his teachings their sins will be forgiven and they will go to heaven. They refer to Jesus as Christ, from the Greek for "Anointed One" (Messiah in Hebrew). Jesus lived in modern-day Israel about 2,000 years ago. After his death his followers formed a community that ultimately gave rise to the Christian Church. The story of Jesus has inspired many artists over the centuries and some of our greatest works of art show episodes from his life.

THE TRINITY

The Trinity, or Holy Trinity, refers to the belief that God is represented as three beings—Father, Son, and Holy Spirit (or Holy Ghost). When Mary found Jesus in the Temple of Jerusalem (see page 14), he referred to the temple as his "Father's house." And when Jesus was baptized (page 16), God said: "This is my Son, whom I love." The Holy Spirit visited Mary when she was told that she would give birth to Jesus (page 8), and came to Jesus at his baptism.

In this detail of a 15th-century painting, the Holy Spirit is represented by a white dove. All three persons of the Trinity wear a halo, or circle of light, to show their holiness.

Matthew, Mark, Luke, and John are represented by their symbols on the cover of this 14th-century lectionary (book of readings from the Bible) above. They surround an almond-shaped ivory plaque of Jesus.

An illustration of a relief carved over the doorway of the church of St Trophime, in Arles, France, in the 12th century. It shows Christ surrounded by symbols of Matthew, Mark, Luke, and John.

THE GOSPELS

The word *gospel* means "good news." It was used by Jesus' followers to describe his teachings and was later adopted to refer to the writings of the evangelists—Matthew, Mark, Luke, and John. Matthew and John were among the original 12 disciples; Mark was a cousin of the disciple Barnabus; and Luke was a member of the early Christian community in Antioch. In Christian art, Matthew is represented by an angel (**a**), Mark by a lion (**b**), Luke by an ox (**c**), and John by an eagle (**d**).

SCENES FROM THE PASSION OF CHRIST
Hans Memling
1470–71
Galleria Sabauda, Turin (Italy)

This work by Hans Memling (c.1430–94) is composed of a series of miniature scenes telling about the Passion (the events leading up to the crucifixion of Jesus, and his resurrection). The artist has chosen to represent the scenes in a medieval European city rather than in Jerusalem. They can be read as a story from top left, where Jesus enters Jerusalem (1). Judas appears with the high priests (2), at the Last Supper (3), and kissing Jesus to betray him (4). The cockerel watches as Peter denies knowing Jesus (5). We see the cross being made (6), before it is carried (7) outside the city to Golgotha, where Jesus is nailed to it (8) and then crucified (9). The entombment (10) and resurrection (11) follow. Memling's patron was Tommaso Portinari, an Italian banker in Bruges, and Portinari (12) and his wife Maria (13) appear in the bottom corners.

In this detail of a French painting from around 1445, God is shown looking down on the scene of the Annunciation. He is the source of the rays of light.

The Annunciation

...God sent the angel Gabriel to Nazareth, a town in Galilee, to a virgin pledged to be married to a man named Joseph… The virgin's name was Mary. …the angel said to her… "You will be with child and give birth to a son, and you are to give him the name Jesus." Luke 1:26–31

In the Christian story, Mary and Joseph were engaged to be married when the archangel Gabriel appeared to Mary and told her that she would give birth to the Son of God. This event is known as the Annunciation. Gabriel told Mary to call the child Jesus, a name that derives from the Hebrew Joshua and means "Jehovah (God) is salvation." The child was conceived through the Holy Spirit and in many paintings the dove representing the Holy Spirit is shown floating down to Mary. The festival commemorating the event is held on March 25, nine months before Christmas Day. The Annunciation is a popular theme in Christian art.

GABRIEL

The archangel Gabriel is God's messenger and a herald of birth. Before visiting Mary, he foretold the birth of John the Baptist (see page 14). Gabriel also appears in the Old Testament, interpreting the prophet Daniel's visions. He is also venerated by Jews and Muslims. In the Muslim Holy Book, the Qur'an, Gabriel (or Jibril) tells Muhammad that he is to be the messenger of God on Earth.

Gabriel is usually shown with beautiful wings, as in this sculpture by the Italian artist Donatello (1386–1466).

The dove represents the Holy Spirit. It is often shown descending from God to Mary on rays of light.

The lily is a symbol of the Virgin's purity. It also shows that the event took place in springtime. In many paintings Gabriel is holding the flower and over time it came to be one of his attributes (a symbol that says who a person is).

SYMBOLS

The three most important elements in paintings on this theme are the archangel Gabriel, the Virgin Mary, and the dove. Many other symbols are associated with the scene, such as the lily, but they vary according to the date of the painting and the particular artist.

Mary is almost always shown with the Bible open before her. According to St. Bernard, she is reading the prophecy from Isaiah 7:14: "The virgin will be with child and will give birth to a son."

In this detail from a 15th-century German painting, the angel's greeting—Ave gratia plena Dominus ("Greetings most famous one. The Lord is with you.") appear on a scroll around his scepter. The words were later used by Roman Catholics as a prayer to Mary, known as "Ave Maria" or "Hail Mary."

ST. COLUMBA ALTARPIECE *(left panel)*
Rogier van der Weyden
c. 1455
Alte Pinakothek, Munich (Germany)

The Flemish artist Rogier van der Weyden (c.1399–64) painted this Annunciation in oil on an oak panel in the mid 1450s. It was part of an altarpiece for the Church of St. Columba, in Cologne. It shows the archangel Gabriel (1) greeting the Virgin Mary (2), who is kneeling at a prie-dieu (3), a wooden stand used for prayer. A flowering lily (4) stands in a pot between the two figures. Gabriel holds a scepter (5), and his words of greeting (in Latin) run across this in the form of a cross, symbolizing Christianity. The dove of the Holy Spirit (6) is borne on rays of light. The altarpiece was celebrated for the slender delicacy of the figures and their graceful movements.

This illustration from a medieval manuscript shows an angel announcing the birth to the shepherds.

The Nativity

So Joseph also went up from the town of Nazareth in Galilee to Judea, to Bethlehem. … He went there … with Mary, who … was expecting a child. While they were there, … she gave birth to her firstborn, a son. She wrapped him in cloths and placed him in a manger, because there was no room for them in the inn.   Luke 2:4–7

The Holy Land was under Roman rule at the time of Jesus' birth and when the emperor Augustus ordered a census everyone had to return to their hometowns to be counted. Joseph and Mary left Nazareth and traveled to Bethlehem. As they arrived, Mary knew that it was time for her baby to be born. They found the inn full, and made their way to a stable in a rough cave. Jesus was born and Mary laid him a manger, or feeding trough, where angels came to announce the birth and to adore him. The Nativity, or birth of Jesus, is a major theme in Christian art. From the 15th century, Jesus was sometimes shown illuminating the scene and lighting up the world.

THE SHEPHERDS
When Jesus was born, an angel appeared to shepherds looking after their flock in a field nearby. At first the simple shepherds were frightened, but when the angel announced the good news, they were delighted. Then a whole host of angels appeared in the night sky, praising God. They encouraged the shepherds to find the baby Jesus and to worship him. The shepherds represent ordinary people, who are astonished and overjoyed to learn of the birth of Jesus.

THE NATIVITY, AT NIGHT
Geertgen tot Sint Jans
1484–90
National Gallery, London (England)

This work by the Dutch artist Geertgen tot Sint Jans (c.1460–90) was one of the earliest to show the nativity scene at night. He has combined two scenes in the painting: in the foreground the baby Jesus (1) glows with a brilliant light which illuminates Mary (2) as she bends forward in prayer, Joseph (3), and five happy little angels (4). Also visible behind the crib are the ox and the ass (5). In the background, the second scene shows the angel (6) as he announces the birth of Jesus to the frightened shepherds (7) with their flocks in the fields. The shepherds are shielding their eyes from the brightness of the angel's light.

Almost all nativity paintings show an ox and an ass in the stable adoring the baby Jesus. This scene from a nativity painting is by the Italian painter Fra Filippo Lippi (c.1406–69).

Adoration of the Magi

After Jesus was born in Bethlehem in Judea, during the time of King Herod, Magi from the East came to Jerusalem and asked, "Where is the one who has been born king of the Jews? We saw his star in the east and have come to worship him." Matthew 2:1–2

The Magi, also known as the Wise Men or the Three Kings, followed a guiding star from the East to bring gifts to the baby Jesus. In Jerusalem, news of the strangers reached King Herod, who was worried about any new "King of the Jews." Herod asked the Magi to let him know where the child was, but they were warned in a dream to leave without telling him. Herod was furious and ordered the slaughter of all baby boys in Bethlehem under two years of age.

This early Christian catacomb graffiti shows the Magi following the star to present Jesus with their gifts of gold, frankincense, and myrrh. Joseph stands behind the seated Mary.

THE MAGI
The Magi were members of a clan of priests in ancient Persia. They practiced astrology and interpreted dreams, and so became known as "wise men." In later tradition, they were called kings and named Caspar, Melchior, and Balthasar. In medieval and Renaissance art, they also came to represent the three regions of the known world—Asia, Africa, and Europe.

THE PRESENTATION IN THE TEMPLE AND THE FLIGHT TO EGYPT
According to Jewish tradition, Mary and Joseph took Jesus to the Temple in Jerusalem, to present him to God (right). While they were there, a devout man named Simeon took the baby in his arms. He blessed the holy family because God had promised him that he would not die before he had seen the Messiah. A prophetess named Anna also approached, thanking God for sending the savior. Soon afterward, an angel appeared to Joseph in a dream and warned him that his family was in danger from King Herod. The angel told him to take Jesus to Egypt. Joseph and his family left at once (above). These scenes are shown on the predella (a painting or series of paintings attached to an altarpiece) of Gentile da Fabriano's altarpiece.

ADORATION OF THE MAGI
Gentile da Fabriano
1423, Uffizi Gallery, Florence (Italy)

This altarpiece was commissioned from the Italian painter Gentile da Fabriano (1370–1427) for the Church of Santa Trinità in Florence. In its ornate frame, the main painting has four scenes. In the first arch (1), the three Magi gaze at the star. In the second (2), they ride toward the gates of Jerusalem. In the third (3), they approach Bethlehem. In the main scene, the Magi and their huge procession arrive at the stable where Jesus was born. The oldest Magus (4) has taken off his crown and kneels before Mary (5) and Jesus (6). The second king (7) kneels, as the third (8) waits his turn. A huge crowd, including exotic animals such as monkeys (9), looks on.

The Debate with the Teachers

They found him in the temple courts, sitting among the teachers, listening to them and asking them questions. Everyone who heard him was amazed at his understanding and his answers. ... His mother said to him, ... "Your father and I have been anxiously searching for you." "Why ... ?" he asked. "Didn't you know I had to be in my Father's house?" Luke 2:46–49

When Jesus was 12 years old, Mary and Joseph took him to Jerusalem to celebrate the spring feast of the Passover. The celebrations went on for a week, commemorating the Israelites' liberation from slavery in Egypt. Making their way back to Nazareth with many other families, Mary suddenly realized that her son was missing. She and Joseph hurried back to Jerusalem, and searched for three days before finally finding Jesus in the Temple. There he was discussing and debating with the Jewish teachers.

THE TEMPLE OF JERUSALEM
The first temple in Jerusalem was built by Solomon around 950 BC. It was made up of a vestibule, a nave, and the inner Holy of Holies. It held the Ark of the Covenant, a wooden chest containing the tablets of the Ten Commandments. This magnificent structure was destroyed by Nebuchadnezzar in 586 BC and later replaced by a new, less majestic building. Around 20 BC the second temple was restored and expanded by King Herod, and it was there that Jesus debated with the teachers. The Temple of Jerusalem was a constant and important symbol of Israel's unity.

A reconstruction of the Temple renovated by King Herod of Judea (37–4 BC).

THE TEACHERS
The men with whom Jesus had a "dispute" (or debate) in the Temple are variously described as teachers, doctors, scholars, and scribes. They were educated men who became the official interpreters of Jewish law. They had great power, teaching the law and serving as judges in the Sanhedrin, the court of justice and supreme council in Jerusalem. They were also associated with the sect of the Pharisees (see page 20).

Left: In his version of Christ Among the Doctors, the German painter Albrecht Dürer (1471–1528) emphasized the contrast between the youthful Jesus and the elderly teachers.

Joseph worked as a humble carpenter. This detail by Dutch painter Robert Campin (c. 1378–1444) shows him in his workshop.

JOSEPH

When Jesus refers to his Father's house, he means the Temple of God the Father. Mary, on the other hand, is referring to the concern of his earthly father, her husband. Joseph, who himself came from the line of King David, certainly cared for Jesus as if he were his father.

THE FINDING OF THE SAVIOR IN THE TEMPLE
William Holman Hunt
1860
City Museum and Art Gallery, Birmingham (England)

In his painting the English painter William Holman Hunt (1827–1910) shows Joseph (1) looking on as Mary (2) puts her arm around Jesus (3), who tightens his belt to show that he is ready to go. One very old teacher (4) holds the sacred Torah scroll (5). He is blind

and feeble and is meant to symbolize the resistance by the Jewish faith to the new teaching. The old teacher is kept free of flies by a child with a whisk (6) and has his traditional *tallith* (7), or fringed prayer shawl. Next to him sits a teacher holding a phylactery (8), a small box containing Hebrew texts. The teachers are being served by a wine-carrier (9) and attended by musicians. One youth holds a sistrum (10), a rattle that originated in ancient Egypt.

JOHN THE BAPTIST

John was the son of Elizabeth, a cousin of the Virgin Mary. His parents were told by the archangel Gabriel that he would become a prophet. He went out to the desert of Judea, where he lived a simple life, surviving on locusts and wild honey. He began baptizing people, saying that he was preparing the way for someone much greater than himself. He meant Jesus, which was why he felt at first that the baptism should be the other way round.

This painted and gilded wooden statue of John the Baptist was created by Donatello in 1438.

The Baptism of Jesus

... Jesus came from Nazareth in Galilee and was baptized by John in the Jordan. As Jesus was coming up out of the water, he saw heaven being torn open and the Spirit descending on him like a dove. And a voice came from heaven: "You are my Son, whom I love; with you I am well pleased."
Mark 1:9–11

John the Baptist dipped people in the Jordan River to show that they repented of their sins and were cleansed of them. Many came out of the towns and villages to see him. One day Jesus came to hear John preach and to be baptized by him. John felt that it was he who should be baptized by Jesus, but was persuaded that this was the way it should be. After the baptism, God spoke to let everyone know that Jesus was his son. The early Christians adopted baptism as a way of showing commitment to Jesus and the Church.

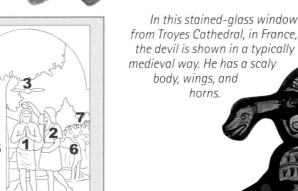

Angels often appear in paintings of the baptism. They hold garments for those being baptized, as in this detail from a painting by Andrea del Verrocchio (c.1435–88), who was assisted by Leonardo da Vinci and Sandro Botticelli.

THE TEMPTATION OF JESUS

After the baptism, Jesus went into the wilderness and fasted for 40 days. At the end of that time, the devil taunted him with three temptations. He tempted Jesus to show he was the Son of God by turning stone into bread, or by leaping from the top of the Temple in Jerusalem. The devil also offered Jesus riches if he would only worship him. Jesus resisted all these temptations.

THE BAPTISM OF CHRIST
Piero della Francesca
c.1450
National Gallery, London (England)

Piero della Francesca (c.1416–92) painted this work for a priory in his hometown of Sansepolcro, in Tuscany. The painting shows Christ (1) standing in the center in the shallow waters of the Jordan River, which have stopped flowing at the moment that he is baptized. John (2), dressed in his camel-hair robe, pours water over Jesus from a shallow bowl. Above Jesus' head, a white dove (3) hovers, representing the Holy Spirit. Three angels (4) attend the baptism, and one holds a pink garment (5) for Jesus. Behind John, a young man (6) disrobes in preparation for his own baptism. The trees and background are typically Tuscan, and the town (7) is thought to be Piero's Sansepolcro. One of the most striking things about this painting is the light that comes from above, creating pastel colors and casting pale shadows.

In this stained-glass window from Troyes Cathedral, in France, the devil is shown in a typically medieval way. He has a scaly body, wings, and horns.

The Transfiguration

… Jesus took with him Peter, James, and John … , and led them up a high mountain by themselves. There he was transfigured before them. His face shone like the sun, and his clothes became as white as the light. **Matthew 17:1–2**

When Jesus was transfigured, he was changed into a more spiritual state. His disciples then saw their Lord in all his radiant glory. At the same time he was joined by two Old Testament prophets, Moses and Elijah. A bright cloud came down from heaven, and God said: "This is my Son, whom I love; listen to him!" The transfiguration showed a significant link between Jesus' spiritual work and the revelations of the Old Testament. It became the subject of the last work by one of the greatest artists of the Renaissance, Raphael. The Transfiguration is commemorated in a church festival, held on August 6.

MOSES AND ELIJAH

Moses was the prophet who led the Israelites out of slavery in Egypt and took them to the borders of the Promised Land. He received the Ten Commandments from God and was the lawgiver of Israel. Elijah was a later Old Testament prophet who attacked the worship of ancient gods such as Baal. He insisted that the Israelites worship the only true God, Jehovah. According to the *Book of Kings*, Elijah was taken up into heaven without dying.

In this sculpture of 1516, the artist Michelangelo has shown Moses with two small horns on his head. This came about because the Hebrew word for "rays of light" was mistranslated as "horns."

The prophet Elijah is often depicted with a raven. During a drought God told Elijah to go to a brook east of the Jordan River. There "ravens brought him bread and meat in the morning and bread and meat in the evening, and he drank from the brook."

CHOOSING THE DISCIPLES

When Jesus began to preach in Galilee, he chose 12 men to be his first apostles, or messengers. The first to be chosen were the brothers Peter and Andrew, who were fishing without success off the shores of the Sea of Galilee. Jesus told them to let their nets down again, and when they did so, they caught so many fish that they could not get them all into their boat. In this way Jesus showed his first disciples how they could help him gather many followers and believers.

Left: This early Christian mosaic from Ravenna, Italy, shows Jesus calling his first two disciples. Jesus said: "Follow me and I will make you fishers of men."

THE TRANSFIGURATION OF CHRIST
Raphael
1517–20
Vatican Pinacoteca, Rome (Italy)

Raffaello Sanzio (1483–1520), known in English as Raphael, was asked to paint this work for a French cathedral. When Raphael died, on his 37th birthday, the Transfiguration was displayed at the head of his coffin. This large work is made up of two parts. In the upper part (shown above), Jesus (1) is shown floating in clothes "as white as the light." The bright cloud behind him (2) is a sign of the presence of God. Jesus is flanked by the grey-bearded Moses (3) and Elijah (4), who represent Old Testament law and prophecy. From the top of the mountain, the disciples (5) James, Peter, and John shield their eyes from the radiance.

THE MARRIAGE AT CANA
Gerard David
c.1500, Louvre, Paris (France)

The Netherlandish painter Gerard David (c.1460–1523) worked mainly in Bruges, where he became the last great master of the Bruges school. In this work, Mary (1) turns to Jesus (2), who is seated at one end of the wedding table. Both are shown with haloes. The bride (3), bridegroom (4), and other guests are dressed in a style contemporary with the artist. Outside we see a Gothic-style church (5), and the wall is hung with a medieval tapestry (6). A monk (7) watches the scene as the wine is presented. The artist's patron (8) and his wife (9) (the people who commissioned the painting) appear in the work, which was usual practice.

JESUS TEACHES HIS FOLLOWERS WITH PARABLES
Throughout the gospels Jesus tells many parables. These simple stories teach a moral lesson through the use of metaphors. Jesus uses scenes from everyday life to illustrate some of his most important teachings. According to Mark, when Jesus spoke to his followers "he did not say anything to them without using a parable." One of the best known parables is the tale of the Prodigal Son (Luke 15:11–32). In this story a man asks his father for his share of his father's estate and leaves for distant lands. After he squanders all of his money he returns to his father to ask his forgiveness.

The First Miracle

Jesus said to the servants, "Fill the jars with water;" so they filled them to the brim. Then he told them, "Now draw some out and take it to the master of the banquet." They did so, and the master … tasted the water that had been turned into wine. John 2:7–9

The New Testament records many occasions when Jesus performed miracles. The first public miracle occurred at the village of Cana, where Jesus and his mother, along with some of the disciples, were invited to a wedding feast. During the banquet Mary noticed that the wine had run out and told her son. Jesus quietly told the servants to fill six large pots with water and then pour some for the master of the banquet. When they did so, the servants were amazed to see that the water had turned into wine.

This 6th-century ivory relief sculpture from Ravenna, Italy, shows a much simpler version of the same scene.

Below: A detail from the painting Return of the Prodigal Son, *by the Italian artist Andrea Palma (1664–1730). The father welcomes his son with an embrace while one of his servants brings him new clothes. In this story Jesus teaches how God, represented in the story by the father, forgives repentant sinners, represented by the son returning to his father.*

WATER INTO WINE

The six stone water jars were kept for the purpose of ceremonial washing. It was a Jewish ritual for tableware to be washed before a meal was served. Guests also washed their hands. According to the Gospel of John, when Jesus turned the water into wine, he performed the first of his many miracles. After seeing this, his disciples put their faith in him. In Christian art, the feasting scene became a favorite subject for refectories (rooms where the monks or nuns ate).

THE ENTRY INTO JERUSALEM

On his way to Jerusalem, Jesus told his disciples where to find a donkey and her foal. Jesus then rode the foal for the last part of his journey. People had heard that Jesus was on his way, and crowds gathered to see him. As shown in the scene above, some onlookers spread their cloaks on the road, while others cut branches from the trees and threw them along the way. This event is celebrated on the Sunday before Easter, called Palm Sunday.

This detail from a 4th-century Sicilian sarcophagus (coffin) shows Jesus riding to Jerusalem.

Below: Detail from the north doors of the Baptistery of Florence showing Jesus expelling the merchants from the Temple. The gilded bronze doors were created by Lorenzo Ghiberti (1378–1455).

The Cleansing of the Temple

... Jesus went up to Jerusalem. In the temple courts he found people selling cattle, sheep, and doves, and others sitting at tables exchanging money. So he made a whip out of cords, and drove all from the temple area ... .
John 2:13–15

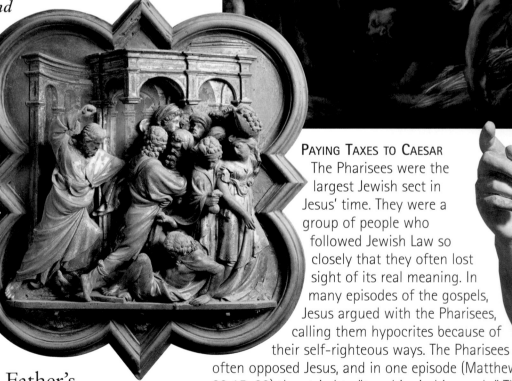

When Jesus arrived at the Temple in Jerusalem he was furious to find that it had been turned into a marketplace. He used a makeshift whip to clear it of traders and their animals, overturning the moneylenders' tables in the process. He told them that his Father's house was a place of prayer, and that they had turned it into a "den of thieves." Jesus' dramatic reaction was not typical of him, but symbolized a wish to do away with old ways.

PAYING TAXES TO CAESAR

The Pharisees were the largest Jewish sect in Jesus' time. They were a group of people who followed Jewish Law so closely that they often lost sight of its real meaning. In many episodes of the gospels, Jesus argued with the Pharisees, calling them hypocrites because of their self-righteous ways. The Pharisees often opposed Jesus, and in one episode (Matthew 22:15–22) they tried to "trap him in his words." They asked him if it was right for one who follows the law of God to follow the law of the state and to pay taxes. In response Jesus asked them to show him a coin, it had the emperor's portrait. Then Jesus said "Give to Caesar what is Caesar's, and to God what is God's."

The Prima Porta statue of Augustus from the early 1st century AD. Jesus was born during the reign of Ceasar Augustus (27 BC–4 AD), Rome's first emperor. Augustus was succeeded by his son, Tiberius.

CHRIST DRIVING THE TRADERS FROM THE TEMPLE
Jacob Jordaens
c.1650
Louvre, Paris (France)

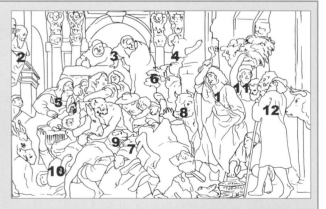

This work by the Flemish artist Jacob Jordaens (1593–1678) is typical of his robust Baroque style, full of dynamic movement and extravagant detail. Strong contrasts of light and shade bring out the hurly-burly of the dramatic scene. Jesus (1), made clearly visible by his deep red cloak, wields his whip. Two pairs of onlookers (2,3) watch the scene from above, while a young man climbs a pillar (4). An old woman grasps a cockerel (5), while one of the doves (6) loses feathers as it flies up. The sheep (7) and oxen (8) were there to be sold to the rich as sacrificial animals, while the pigeons were for the poor. There is even a dog (9) in the scene. A moneylender (10) falls backward, his coins scattered on the floor. The fruit-seller with a basket on her head (11) appears amused, while an old man with a stick (12) looks outraged. Although Matthew says that the episode took place in the Temple precincts (just outside the Temple), most paintings show an interior scene. The animals were sold as sacrificial beasts. During the Reformation the incident prefigured Luther's condemnation of the selling of indulgences.

The Passion

Jesus said, "... Now is the time for judgment on this world; now the prince of this world will be driven out. But I, when I am lifted up from the earth, will draw all people to myself."
John 12:30–32

Jesus predicted his own betrayal and death. The next, most important period of his time on earth is called the Passion (meaning "suffering"). This refers to Jesus' sufferings from the time he entered Jerusalem to his crucifixion and resurrection. The Passion is commemorated each year during Holy Week (Easter). The separate events have been well documented by artists. At the beginning of the 14th century, an Italian artist included all of them on a magnificent altarpiece for Siena Cathedral.

MAESTÀ, back panels
Duccio di Buoninsegna
1308–11
Museo dell'Opera del Duomo, Siena (Italy)

15	16	19		22	23	26
14	17	18	20	21	24	25
1	2	5	7	8	11	12
	3	4	6	9	10	13

Duccio (c.1255–1319) painted these panels on the back of the great altarpiece called Maesta ("Majesty"). They show 26 scenes from the Passion. Entry into Jerusalem (1). Jesus washes his disciples' feet (2). The

A detail of the Maestà showing Jesus washing the feet of a disciple. Before the Last Supper Jesus washed the feet of his disciples to show them that they must serve others as he had served them.

Last Supper (3). Christ tells the disciples that he will soon be leaving them (4). Judas takes 30 silver coins to betray Jesus (5). In the Garden of Gethsemane (6). Jesus is arrested (7). Before high priest Annas (8). Peter denies knowing Jesus (9). Before chief priest Caiaphas (10). Jesus is mocked (11). Jesus is accused by the Pharisees (12). Before Pontius Pilate, the Roman governor of Judea (13). Before King Herod (14). Before Pilate for a second time (15). Jesus is flogged (16). A crown of thorns is placed on his head (17). Pilate washes his hands to show that is not responsible (18). On the way to Golgotha, a hill outside Jerusalem (19). The Crucifixion (20). Christ's body is taken down from the cross (21). Jesus is buried (22). The three Marys (the mother of Jesus, the wife of Cleopas, and Mary Magdalene) see an angel at the empty tomb (23). Jesus descends into hell to set his forefathers free (24). Jesus appears to Mary Magdalene (25). Two disciples meet Jesus on the road to Emmaus (26).

In this detail of Duccio's Maestà, Judas Iscariot, who had agreed to hand Jesus over to the high priests to arrest him, betrays him with a kiss (see page 25). To the left, one of Jesus' disciples cuts off the ear of one of the high priests' servants.

THE LAST SUPPER
Leonardo da Vinci
c.1495–97 Refectory of Santa
Maria delle Grazie, Milan (Italy)

The Last Supper shows Jesus (1) seated at the center of a long table. He is reaching out toward the wine (2) and the bread (3). The gesture suggests the first celebration of an important Christian sacrament called the Eucharist, or Holy Communion. This took place at the Last Supper when Jesus gave his disciples bread saying, "This is my body" and wine saying, "This is my blood." The 12 disciples are seated on either side of Jesus. Leonardo has divided them into four groups of three. Judas (4), the traitor, is leaning on his right elbow and reaching out toward a piece of bread. Jesus has just announced that one of them will betray him, and the disciples are reacting in surprise and dismay. James the Great (5) has his mouth open in astonishment, while Peter (6) is holding a dagger which he will use at dawn to cut off the ear of Malchus, one of the soldiers arresting Jesus. John (7), the favorite, is seated on Jesus' right, in the place of honor.

THE EUCHARIST
The Christian ceremony of the Eucharist, celebrated during church services, commemorates the Last Supper. The host (a piece of bread or wafer) and wine are distributed to the congregation by a priest in memory of Jesus' last meal with his disciples.

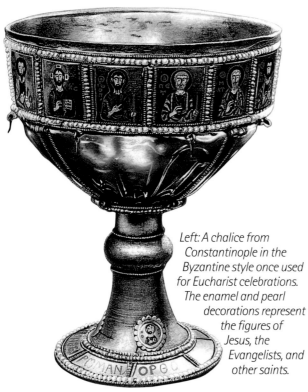

Left: A chalice from Constantinople in the Byzantine style once used for Eucharist celebrations. The enamel and pearl decorations represent the figures of Jesus, the Evangelists, and other saints.

The Last Supper

... Jesus was reclining at the table with the Twelve. And while they were eating, he said, "I tell you the truth, one of you will betray me." They were very sad and began to say to him one after the other, "Surely not I, Lord?"   Matthew 26:20–22

The Last Supper was the final meal that Jesus had with the disciples in Jerusalem before he was arrested. The event was seen as immensely important by later Christians, and became the subject of many works of art. These were often painted as frescoes on the walls of religious communities' refectories. This was the case with the famous fresco by Leonardo da Vinci (1452–1519). Unfortunately it soon began to deteriorate and has been restored many times.

THE BETRAYAL

Jesus had told believers to expect betrayal and persecution. Nevertheless, it was a devastating moment when he told the 12 disciples that one of them was a traitor. Leonardo da Vinci chose to portray this moment and show real human reactions on the part of his disciples. He achieved this by representing emotional gestures and facial expressions. Other artists placed Judas Iscariot on the other side of the table, alone, with his back to the spectator. Some even portrayed a later moment, after Judas had slipped away. According to the Gospels, Judas Iscariot had made an arrangement with the high priests before the meal; "The one I kiss is the man; arrest him and lead him away under guard" (Mark 14:44). Some time after the last meal Judas Iscariot lead the high priests to where Jesus was praying with the other disciples. In return, the high priests paid Judas Iscariot 30 silver coins.

The Spanish painter Juan de Juanes (c. 1523–79) chose to separate Judas from the other disciples. Juanes, son of the painter Vicente Macip, was the leading artist of his time in Valencia.

INRI became a traditional representation in art for the inscription placed over Jesus' head. It stood for Iesus Nazarenus Rex Iudaeorum (Jesus of Nazareth, King of the Jews). The nesting pelican was a symbol of charity, or love of humankind. Legend said that the bird fed its young with its own blood.

The Crucifixion

They brought Jesus to the place called Golgotha (which means The Place of the Skull). Then they offered him wine mixed with myrrh, but he did not take it. And they crucified him. ... The written notice of the charge against him read: THE KING OF THE JEWS. They crucified two robbers with him, one on his right and one on his left. Those who passed by hurled insults at him...

Mark 15:22–26

The Jewish ruling council and chief priests found Jesus guilty of blasphemy by claiming to be the Son of God. The Roman governor, Pontius Pilate, refused to take responsibility for what happened to Jesus and finally handed him over to be executed. Jesus was crucified along with two thieves. The Crucifixion has been shown in many different ways in Christian art. Sometimes it is depicted in all its horror and sadness.

Medieval writers suggested that the crucifixion site was also the burial place of Adam, the first man. A skull therefore represented Adam. The ointment jar may have referred to the symbolic washing away of Adam's sin.

DESCENT FROM THE CROSS

Joseph of Arimathea, who was a member of the Jewish ruling council and a secret disciple, asked Pilate for permission to bury Jesus. Nicodemus, a Pharisee who had also become a believer, helped Joseph take the body down from the cross. The two men washed the body and wrapped it in strips of linen. In this painting of *The Deposition* by Raphael (below), the body of Jesus is carried away in the presence of the Virgin Mary, her female companions, and John. The body was taken to a nearby garden and placed in a new tomb cut into rock.

THE CRUCIFIXION
Jan van Eyck and workshop assistant
c.1430
Metropolitan Museum of Art, New York

This painting by Van Eyck (c.1395–1441) and an assistant shows Jesus (1) nailed to a tau-cross (shaped like a letter T), just as his right side is being pierced by a spear. The soldier (2) holding the spear, who is perhaps blind, is guided by a bystander. Above the cross, the inscription (3) appears in Hebrew, Latin, and Greek. The repentant thief (4) is to the right, or "good" side of Jesus, while the unrepentant thief (5) is to the left, "evil" side. In the sky, the moon (6) represents the Old Testament. Another soldier has just offered Jesus a sponge (7) soaked in vinegar. The spear-bearer and sponge-bearer symbolize the Church and the Synagogue respectively. The Virgin Mary (8) is comforted by John (9), while Mary Magdalene (10) looks up at Jesus.

The Resurrection

Thomas touches Jesus' wounds in this medieval illustration.

... The women ... went to the tomb, but when they entered, they did not find the body of the Lord Jesus. ... Two men in clothes that gleamed like lightning ... said to them, "Why do you look for the living among the dead? He is not here; he has risen!" Luke 24:1–6

On the third day after his death on the cross, Jesus rose again. The events of Jesus' resurrection are described in various ways in the gospels. In some versions, the tomb is guarded by soldiers. The Jewish chief priests had asked for this, so that the disciples could not steal the body and claim that Jesus had risen. In John's Gospel, Mary Magdalene meets the risen Jesus, who later also appeared to the disciples. After Jesus had ascended to heaven, the disciples continued to spread his gospel and founded the Christian Church.

JESUS APPEARS TO HIS DISCIPLES

The resurrected Jesus made a number of appearances to his disciples. Cleopas and a friend met him on the way home to Emmaus, but only realized who he was when he broke bread, blessed it, and gave it to them. This showed that those who took part in Communion would experience Jesus' presence. Jesus also appeared to the disciples, and later to Thomas, who had doubted his friends' story.

In this painting by Rembrandt (1606–69), the two disciples sitting with Jesus have a dawning awareness of who he really is.

A 12th-century enamel of the Ascension by the metalworker Nicholas of Verdun.

RESURRECTION (panel of the Isenheim Altarpiece)
Matthias Grünewald
c.1515
Musée d'Unterlinden, Colmar (France)

In this painting the German artist Grünewald (c.1470–1528) chose to show the resurrection as a form of ascension. We see Jesus (1) floating in the air, rising up from his shrouds, above an open sarcophagus (2). He holds his hands up to show the marks (3) of the nails, and the spear wound (4), and nail marks on his feet (5) are also clearly visible. Jesus emanates a light which forms a halo (6) of brilliant color and illuminates the whole scene. Armed and armored guards (7) turn away or shield their eyes from the dazzling aura. Grünewald was masterful at painting colored light, and his altarpiece is a very important work of German Renaissance painting.

THE ASCENSION

Forty days after his resurrection, Jesus was taken up into heaven before the disciples' eyes. As they stood on the Mount of Olives and watched Jesus rise into the sky, a cloud hid him from their sight. Then suddenly two men dressed in white appeared next to the disciples. "Why do you stand here looking into the sky?" they asked. "This same Jesus, who has been taken from you into heaven, will come back in the same way."

The Life of Jesus

The Angel Gabriel appears to Mary.

Jesus is born in Bethlehem.

The visit of the shepherds and the magi.

Jesus is brought to the Temple.

Joseph takes Mary and the baby Jesus to Egypt.

Joseph, Mary, and Jesus return to Nazareth.

Mary and Joseph find Jesus in the Temple debating with the doctors.

Jesus is baptized by John the Baptist.

Jesus is tempted by the devil in the desert.

Jesus calls his first disciples and begins his ministry.

Jesus performs his first miracle.

Jesus is transfigured before three of his disciples.

Jesus enters into Jerusalem and drives the merchants from the Temple.

Judas agrees to betray Jesus.

Jesus washes the disciples' feet and at the Last Supper predicts his betrayal.

Jesus prays in Garden of Gethsemane.

Jesus is betrayed by Judas and arrested.

Jesus is brought before the high priests.

Peter denies knowing Jesus.

Jesus is brought before Pilate and Herod.

Soldiers mock Jesus, Pilate orders his crucifixion.

Jesus is taken to Golgotha and is crucified.

Jesus is buried.

The Resurrection.

The risen Jesus appears to his disciples.

The Ascension, Jesus is taken up to heaven.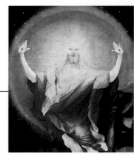

Historical Time Line

23 BC	Augustus Caesar becomes emperor of Rome	4 BC	Death of King Herod		Caesar, reign of Tiberius begins	28 AD	Herod orders the execution of John the Baptist
		6 AD	Romans appoint procurators to govern Judea, a province of Rome	26 AD	Pontius Pilate named procurator of Judea		
37 BC	Herod becomes king of Judea					30 AD	Pontius Pilate orders the crucifixion of Jesus
7–6 BC	birth of Jesus	14 AD	Death of Augustus	27 AD	John the Baptist baptizes Jesus		

Artists' Biographies

Gerard David (born c.1460, Oudewater, died 1523, Bruges) received his early training as a painter in Haarlem. He later went to Bruges and studied the works of Jan van Eyck, Rogier van der Weyden, Hugo van der Goes, and Hans Memling. David became famous painting several rich and colorful altarpieces and filled the position formerly held by Memling as the official painter of Bruges. David is considered the last of the great masters of the Bruges school.

Duccio di Buoninsegna (born c.1255, Siena, died c.1319, Siena) is considered the founder of the Siennese school. Little is known about his life and career. In 1308 Duccio received his greatest commission from the newly rebuilt Siena cathedral, the *Maestà* altarpiece. Duccio's style combined elements of Byzantine art (art of the Eastern Roman Empire, 330–1453 AD) with Italian medieval style. Duccio influenced generations of artists with his elegant, graceful style.

Geertgen Tot Sint Jans (born c. 1465, Leiden, died c.1495, Haarlem), whose name means "Little Gerard of the Knights of St. John," lived with a religious order of the Knights of St. John in Haarlem. Very little is known about his life and career. Many of his works are now lost. His altarpiece of the Crucifixion, painted for the Knights of St. John, is considered his masterpiece. Only two side panels of this work survive.

Gentile da Fabriano (born c.1370, Fabriano, died 1427, Rome), originally named Gentile di Niccolò di Giovanni di Massio, was one of the painters of the International Gothic style, an elegant, delicate style which spread across Western Europe between c.1375 and 1425. His surviving masterpiece, the *Adoration of the Magi* altarpiece, influenced many Florentine artists of the time. His rich, decorative style, marked by the lavish use of gold, provided a contrast to the stark realism of other artists working in Florence at the time.

Matthias Grünewald (born c.1480, Würzburg, died 1528, Halle), whose real name is Mathis Neithart Gothart, was one of the leading artists of the Renaissance in Germany. His masterpiece, known as the Isenheim altarpiece, was commissioned in 1512 for the hospital chapel of St. Anthony's Monastery in Isenheim (France). Grünewald's work, previously mistakenly attributed to another German Renaissance artist, Albrecht Dürer, has been rediscovered by scholars and his way of portraying realistic scenes is now considered one of the most expressive.

William Holman Hunt (born 1827, London, died 1910, London) began his training at the Royal Academy Schools. The ideals of art critic John Ruskin, who called artists to paint in the style of the late Middle Ages and early Renaissance (before the time of the Italian artist Raphael), interested Hunt a great deal. Together with other painters in his circle, he founded the Pre-Raphaelite movement. Hunt's personal interest in the Bible and his religious beliefs motivated him to paint many religious subjects. He visited the Holy Land and studied locations which later became settings for many of his paintings.

Jacob Jordaens (born 1593, Antwerp, died 1678, Antwerp) established a workshop in his hometown. Peter Paul Rubens, the leading painter in Antwerp at the time, hired him as an assistant and Jordaens' style was greatly inspired by him. Jordaens worked on many paintings with religious, mythological, and historical subjects. He also painted portraits and subjects from folklore (fables, proverbs, and tales). After Rubens' death, he became the leading painter in Antwerp, receiving numerous and important commissions.

Leonardo da Vinci (born 1452, Vinci, died 1519, Amboise), one of the geniuses of the Italian Renaissance, was a skilled painter, draftsman, sculptor, architect, and engineer. During his career Leonardo traveled all over Italy. He painted the *Last Supper* in Milan, where he also served the duke as chief engineer and as an architect. He painted several portraits, among which the *Mona Lisa* is the most famous. Leonardo spent the last years of his life in Amboise, France in the service of King Francis I.

Hans Memling (born c.1435 Seligenstadt, died 1494, Bruges) probably studied painting in Cologne, Germany. Sometime in the late 1450's he moved to Brussels, where he was apprenticed to the painter Rogier van der Weyden. Later, he settled in Bruges and became a leading Flemish painter. Memling's style is related to that of contemporary Flemish painters such as Jan van Eyck, Dieric Bouts, Hugo van der Goes, and Rogier van der Weyden.

Piero della Francesca (born c.1416, Sansepolcro, died 1492, Sansepolcro) was born in a small town in central Italy but spent many years working in important artistic centers, such as Urbino and Arezzo. He also spent some years of his youth in Florence where he developed his special style of painting characterized by sharp color, brilliant light, and an accurate use of perspective (a method of representing objects on a flat surface so that they appear to have depth). Piero also wrote two books about geometry and perspective.

Raffaello Sanzio (born 1483, Urbino, died 1520, Rome), is also called Raphael in English. His hometown was an important Italian Renaissance center of culture and learning. In his youth, Raphael was apprenticed to the painter Perugino in Perugia. He later went to Florence where he studied the work of Leonardo da Vinci and Michelangelo. In 1508 he was summoned by the pope to Rome, where he spent the last 12 years of his life. Raphael was commissioned to decorate many rooms of the Vatican Palace and was later appointed the chief architect. He died at the age of 37 and was highly praised by the papal court.

Rogier van der Weyden (born c.1399, Tournai, died 1464, Brussels), was one of the most influential Renaissance painters in northern Europe. He began his career in Tournai, then moved to Brussels where he became the city's official painter in 1437. In the following years he received many commissions to paint both religious and secular subjects. The last years of his life were very successful and his style set the standards for later artists.

Jan van Eyck (born c.1395, Maaseik, died 1441, Bruges), considered the founder of the Flemish school, perfected the art of oil painting. Little is known about his early work because the only paintings attributed to him belong to the later part of his life. The Ghent Altarpiece, consisting of 20 panels, is his most famous work. Jan van Eyck was the first Flemish artist to sign his paintings.

Index

Acknowledgments

The Publishers would like to thank the following museums and picture libraries for the photos used in this book.

Scala Group, Florence: 1, 4–5, 6–7, 8, 10, 10–11, 12 bottom right, 14, 16, 16–17, 18–19, 19, 20, 20–21, 22–23, 25 bottom right, 27
   right, 28, 29

Electa Mondadori, Milan: 24-25

The National Gallery Picture Library, London: 9

Farabola Foto / The Bridgeman Art Library, Milan: 6, 7, 12–13

The Metropolitan Museum of Art, Fletcher Fund, 1993 (33.92a) photograph ©1998 The Metropolitan Museum of Art,
   New York: 3, 26–27

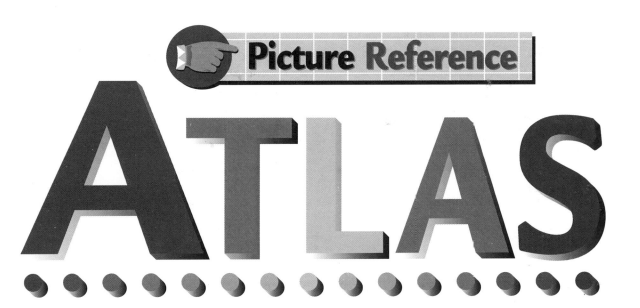

Picture Reference

ATLAS

MEL PICKERING

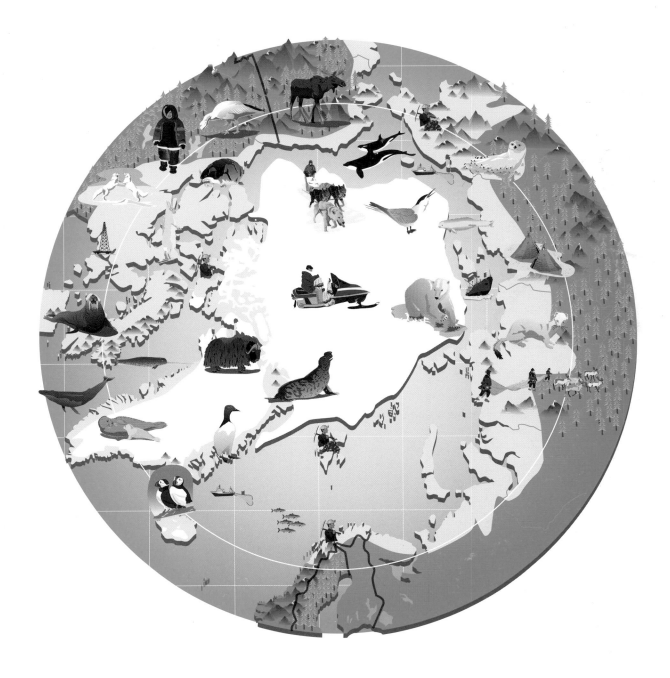

WORLD BOOK / TWO-CAN

Text Andrew Solway
Consultant Steve Watts
Computer illustrations Mel Pickering, Jacqueline Land
Editors Deborah Kespert, Kate Asser
Editorial support Claire Llewellyn, Julia Hillyard, Claire Yude
Art director Belinda Webster
Senior designer Helen Holmes
Photographic credits Zefa p7, John Englefield p9

First published in the United States in 1996 by
World Book, Inc.
525 W. Monroe
20th Floor
Chicago
IL USA 60661
in association with Two-Can Publishing Ltd.

Copyright © Two-Can Publishing Ltd., 1996

**For information on other Word Book products,
call 1-800-255-1750, x 2238.**

ISBN: 0-7166-1746-3 (pbk.)
ISBN: 0-7166-1745-5 (hbk.)
LC: 96-60464

Printed in Hong Kong

1 2 3 4 5 6 7 8 9 10 99 98 97 96